Original title:
Orchid Obsessions

Copyright © 2025 Creative Arts Management OÜ
All rights reserved.

Author: Dorian Ashford
ISBN HARDBACK: 978-1-80581-828-1
ISBN PAPERBACK: 978-1-80581-355-2
ISBN EBOOK: 978-1-80581-828-1

The Language of Delicate Blooms

In whispers soft, they start to talk,
Petals giggle as they start to gawk.
What secrets lie in fragrant air?
Leave your worries, come and share!

A flower's dance, a silly plight,
They sway around, oh what a sight!
With colors bright, they tease the bees,
As butterflies shout, "Can I join, please?"

Faded Dreams and Colorful Hues

The blooms sigh softly, a pastel tone,
Wishing for rain, feeling all alone.
Dancing under the moonlit skies,
Yet giggling on the surface, no need for cries.

In faded dreams, their colors play,
They paint the world in a funny way.
With every petal, a chuckle or two,
Who knew gardening could be so askew?

Tangled Vines of Desire

Vines twist and turn with silly flair,
They climb high, searching for fresh air.
In games of tag, they often lose,
Getting tangled, oh what a ruse!

They reach for light, but bump in between,
Causing chaos, a leafy scene.
Laughing loudly, they just don't care,
In their own world, they find repair.

A Garden of Hidden Yearnings

In a garden where secrets bloom,
Petals hide dreams, while the bees zoom.
A yearning glance amidst the leaves,
A floral comedy that never deceives.

They flirt with sunbeams, oh so bright,
Swaying along in sheer delight.
Hidden wishes under their hue,
Is it love or just morning dew?

A Field of Fantasies

In a garden green and bright,
Flowers giggle with delight,
Petals dancing in the breeze,
Whispering secrets with such ease.

Bees can't help but join the fun,
Buzzing round until they're done,
Each bloom turns to say hello,
Like a party, don't you know?

They wear hats of bright, bold hues,
Sporting colors, mixing crews,
With each twist and cheeky stare,
Whoever knew blooms could have flair?

But mind the scent, it's quite a treat,
Too much laughter at their feet,
A floral frolic, laugh and cheer,
In this wild garden, joy is near!

Sultry Shadows

In sultry gardens where shadows play,
Petals gossip, come what may,
"Do you think we'll have a ball?
Or will the sun make us all fall?"

Leaves are fanning, feeling fine,
Sipping dew like aged wine,
With every flutter, whispers rise,
As if the petals conspire in disguise.

Who wore the best shade of pink?
Or is that just our way to wink?
They tease the breeze, with every sway,
Chasing gold with shades of gray.

A friday night under the moon,
Where blooms and laughter play a tune,
Oh, what a sight, a comical crew,
Who knew flowers could party too?

Swaying Stems

Swaying stems in the silly sun,
Bouncing around just for fun,
With roots that giggle and laugh aloud,
They're the quirkiest folks in any crowd.

Buds poke eyes and petals tease,
As they wiggle in the gentle breeze,
Dancing with such zest and zeal,
An unexpected floral reel.

"Do you think we'll win a prize?
Best in bloom, oh what a surprise!"
A contest of capers, pranks galore,
Every blossom wants just a bit more.

In this garden, joy unfolds,
With every petal, a story told,
Laughter blooms where none were meant,
In swaying stems, time is well spent!

Tending to the Heart's Garden

I watered all my flowers, once or twice,
But now they grow like weeds, oh how nice!
I thought I'd find romance in pots of soil,
But trips to the shop just add to my toil.

With trowels and spades, I dig in with glee,
Yet somehow those roots are just nachos for me!
I talk to my blooms, they're my best friends,
But sadly they don't know where the humor ends.

Beauty Beneath the Surface

I peek beneath the leaves, what do I see?
A hidden dance party, just the bugs and me.
They flutter and jive on my fertile ground,
While I trip on a shovel, tumble straight down.

The petals are bright, but the mess is a blast,
So who cares if my pruning skills aren't unsurpassed?
Each sprout and floret has a laugh in store,
Until they all chirp, 'We're outta here, for sure!'

Colors of the Secret Garden

In a field of hues, I plant my dreams,
Yet the colors all fade—are they rosy or creams?
The blue ones protest, the reds start to pout,
While yellows debate if they're in or out.

I offered them snacks, a buffet of greens,
But they're fussing and fretting like queens and their means.
With petals that wrinkle, their patience wears thin,
Next thing I know, they're hosting a chagrin.

Veils of Aesthetic Longing

Amidst the lush veil, I wander, perplexed,
What's that smell? Is it love or an insect vexed?
The ferns whisper low, with secrets they keep,
While I trip over roots that scream "Kiss the sweep!"

With humor in blooms, I dance on their charms,
But watch out! Here comes a bee who means harms!
I giggle and yell, 'Not my type, if you please!'
As petals erupt like a fit of the tease.

Scented Bonds of Desire

In a garden lush and bright,
Where flowers flirt in day and night,
He caught a whiff, oh joy divine,
Did he just smell that? Oh, it's wine!

The blooms were winking, quite a tease,
Stirring loyalty like the bees,
I promised him my love sincere,
But it was mostly for the beer!

A Palette of Dreamlike Hues

In shades of pink and purple flare,
Dancing petals without a care,
Each color less like art, more play,
Like toddlers gone wild in ballet!

The hues began to scheme and plot,
To paint the world and snatch a pot,
They giggled loud with each new hue,
'Why choose just one when we can do two?'

Caressed by Nature's Touch

The flowers whispered sweet and low,
'Come closer friend, don't be so slow,'
But bees were buzzing, rather rude,
Messy, yet the perfect mood!

A gentle breeze, oh what delight,
As petals waved in sheer delight,
'It's a dance-off!' one bloom declared,
While nature laughed, completely unscared!

The Allure Beneath the Surface

Beneath the leaves, a secret laugh,
Where roots are tangled, what a gaffe!
Did nature plan this silly mess?
Or was she swiping left... no stress!

The blooms conspired, yet gave no clues,
Is it for love or just to snooze?
They hid their charms from watchful eyes,
While beneath them, the soil sighs!

The Dance of the Elegant Flora

In a garden full of grace,
The flowers wiggle in their place,
With petals that just can't behave,
They throw a party, oh so rave!

They don their best in colors bright,
Each bloom trying to outshine the night,
Some twirl and spin, others prance,
As bees gather 'round for a chance!

Obsession in Every Shade

In hues from purple to electric lime,
They gossip and chuckle, oh so sublime,
One said, 'I'm the prettiest you see!'
The others shout, 'No, that's just me!'

A splash of pink with a touch of blue,
Competing for attention, it's quite the zoo,
Petals clash, their banter's quite a show,
In the realm of flowers, it's a dramatic flow!

Blooms Beneath the Moonlight

When moonlight hits each flower's face,
They dance together in a wild embrace,
The night is young, the fragrance sweet,
As critters join in with tiny feet!

One bloom winks at the curious bee,
'Think you're the star? Oh, just wait and see!'
Under the night, petals begin to glow,
A party unfolds, put on a show!

Perfume of the Exotic

Spellbinding scents drift through the air,
A potion brewed with quite a flair,
They say to bees, 'Come get a whiff!'
As they buzz around, feeling the shift!

Each blossom claims it's the finest, true,
'Oh, please smell me, here's my debut!'
With fragrances battling for the crown,
Even the wind's in on this frown!

Garden of Velvet Dreams

In a garden, where petals play,
Lavender whispers joke all day.
Daisies giggle, lilies prance,
Everyone's invited to this dance.

The sun shines bright, oh what a sight,
Bees wear shades, they're feeling right.
Tulips tell puns, oh so sweet,
The daffodils can't help but beat.

Worms in sunglasses hide from sun,
While the vegetables have their fun.
Roses rolling on the ground,
In this garden, joy is found.

A playful breeze twirls leaves of green,
Nature's laughter is truly seen.
With every bloom bringing a jest,
In this garden, we're all blessed.

Secrets in the Silk

A silky secret held so tight,
Buds wearing gowns of pure delight.
With whispers sweet, they softly scheme,
Inviting all into their dream.

Peeking petals, oh so sly,
Stirring mischief as they lie.
Frilly fronds with a cheeky grin,
Tip-toeing where the fun begins.

Funny ants trotting in a line,
Critter parties, oh how divine!
The fragrance floats, tickling the nose,
Laughter blooms as friendship grows.

In the hush of the sly moonlight,
Silken secrets make the night bright.
Where blooms reveal what hides within,
A garden giggle that draws you in.

Dance of the Rare Blooms

In the moonlight, petals twirl,
A quirky dance begins to swirl.
Each bloom dressing up to impress,
Chasing sunbeams in a wild dress.

Cacti sway with a prickly grace,
Soft petals bounce, keeping pace.
The violets spin in bright delight,
Under the stars, they shine so bright.

Pansies giggle, oh what a sight,
With bees that buzz in sheer delight.
A dandelion flips in the breeze,
Creating chaos with utmost ease.

At the stroke of midnight's charm,
Even weeds weave without alarm.
In this dance, all feel the thrill,
Rare blooms sparkle, bending will.

Fragrance of Desire

A wafting scent of silly thrill,
In the garden where laughter spills.
Petals flirting, oh what a tease,
With honeyed breezes, they aim to please.

Pollen parties on dew-kissed nights,
So many colors, so many lights.
Each bloom's a riddle, each stem a joke,
The garden's filled with giggles and smoke.

The fragrance of fun fills the air,
Bringing all critters, that's only fair.
Jasmine whispers tales from above,
In the land where blooms share their love.

Every inhale, a joyous cheer,
Fragrant moments we hold so dear.
In this garden of scented desire,
We dance, we laugh, and never tire.

Captured by Iridescence

In a pot I spy a sight,
Colors dancing, pure delight.
Winked at me with petals bright,
Hoping I won't skip the light.

Watered dreams in every hue,
With laughter, they all grew.
Twirling 'round, a floral crew,
In the sunshine, they debut.

Friends think I've lost my mind,
Chatting blooms, oh, how unkind!
Telling tales of love entwined,
Plotting schemes in drawn-out grind.

Yet in this crazed affair of glee,
I find joy just sipping tea.
With oddball blooms surrounding me,
Life's a wacky melody.

The Allure of a Sun-Kissed Bloom

Caught in the warm embrace of light,
She flaunts her colors, oh, what a sight!
Spinning tales where petals write,
A comedy in floral height.

Every morning, I greet the day,
With all my blooms, we laugh and play.
They whisper secrets in a sway,
At times I think they've gone astray.

Sun-kissed whispers tickle my ear,
They boast of romances, bold and clear.
Yet when I join, it's all in fear,
For blooms can tease, but roots hold dear.

No matter how they twist and turn,
In every laugh, a fuss I learn,
With sun-kissed blooms, my heart they churn,
For chaos, I will always yearn.

Secrets Wrapped in Greenery

In a jungle of pots, I roam around,
Where leafy friends make quite the sound.
Whispering secrets, joyfully bound,
In their green, strange joys are found.

They plot mischief when I'm away,
A dance-off that they wish to play.
Each leaf a mask, in green ballet,
I can't help but join the fray.

With twirls of ferns, and giggles loud,
They steal my heart, making me proud.
In nature's whispers, all's allowed,
As laughter blooms within the crowd.

Wrapped in greenery, fun abounds,
Radio on, we make strange sounds.
I never thought that joy compounds,
With leafy pals and silly rounds.

Blooming Echoes of Solitude

In my quiet nook, they spread their cheer,
Petals chatter, no thought of fear.
Echoes of laughter, crystal clear,
They keep me company, drawing near.

Alone but not lonely, they parade,
In colorful hues, a fragrant brigade.
With jests and japes, they serenade,
In solitude, our worlds cascade.

Conversations with blooms, I boast,
Sipping tea, they raise a toast.
To blossomed joys, I'm just a host,
Funny little friends, I love the most.

In silence, we create our song,
With giggles, we join the throng.
These blooming echoes all day long,
In solitude, where we belong.

Secrets Beneath Sunlit Leaves

In the garden under sunny rays,
Petals giggle, shifting ways.
Butterflies dance with silly flair,
While bees play tag without a care.

Lurking roots weave tales of woe,
Of lost socks and seeds that won't grow.
Worms hum tunes to pass the time,
While snails slide by, committing a crime.

Sunlight teases with warm delight,
Catch a glimpse—oh! What a sight!
A rabbit joins the joyful spree,
Bouncing through in glee and glee.

What secrets hide in leafy greens?
Perhaps the craziest of dreams!
Laughter blooms in pots so bright,
In the sunlight, pure delight.

A Garden of Deluding Dreams

In a jungle, grand and spry,
Planted hopes just standing by.
A gnome laughs with cheeky glee,
As squirrels whisper plans to flee.

Tangled vines twist and weave,
Playing tricks that few believe.
A lizard wears a sunhat grand,
Claiming it's the finest brand.

Raindrops tickle leaves so green,
In this place, strange sights are seen.
A dragonfly fee-fi-fo-fum,
Prances 'round—a true charmer, yum!

Blooms wink, as if in jest,
While the tulips puff their chest.
In this garden, dreams take flight,
With a chuckle and pure delight.

Embrace of the Blooms

Petals twirl in breezy cheer,
Whispering jokes for all to hear.
A sunflower spins and sways,
Laughing through the sunny days.

In the shade, a bench does sigh,
As squirrels leap and bumble by.
Floral scents play hide and seek,
Tickling noses, oh so sleek!

Morning glories stretch with grace,
Gossiping about the space.
A hedgehog dreams of flower pies,
While daisies sport their silly ties.

When shadows dance and laughter blooms,
Each critter shines as nature's grooms.
In the embrace of vibrant hue,
Life's just a jest, made for you.

Fragrant Murmurs of the Night

Under starlight, whispers crawl,
Frogs make jokes, and owls call.
Jasmine scents the evening tale,
As crickets chirp a funny scale.

Moonbeams chuckle, soft and sly,
Tickling petals with a shy sigh.
Fireflies light up the dance floor,
While garden shadows beg for more.

Tulips don pajamas bright,
Staying up to share the night.
Nectar flows, laughter high,
In this realm where giggles lie.

When dawn awakens, plants will bloom,
Chasing echoes to chase the gloom.
With fragrant murmurs, dreams take flight,
In a world alive with light.

Echoes in the Greenhouse

In a room where blossoms sway,
Laughter tickles every day.
Pollen whispers silly schemes,
Petals giggle in sunbeams.

Watering cans dance a jig,
While pots complain, 'We're all too big!'
Ferns roll their eyes at every joke,
As cacti poke fun, feeling woke.

Dreams of gardens full of cheer,
Menagerie of blooms so dear.
But watch your step, don't slip and fall,
On those upturned pots that talk and call!

Fantasia of Flora

A rose once wore a party hat,
While violets danced like cats.
Sunflowers spun in wild delight,
Chasing shadows, what a sight!

Daisies giggled, taking a bow,
'Who knew plants could party now?'
With leafy limbs, they did the twist,
Promising fun was hard to resist.

Petunias pranked the weary bee,
Wearing stripes, 'You can't catch me!'
In this green galore of cheer,
Every bloom has stories to share.

The Heart's Bloom

A hapless bud, it took a chance,
To sprout and find the perfect dance.
Daffodils, they wink and sway,
As bees buzz in a funny ballet.

A tulip tried to tell a joke,
But petals curled, the punchline broke.
Yet laughter filled the garden air,
With every bloom beyond compare!

Lilies waving, 'Come join us here!'
In this pot of glee, no fear.
For every heart that dares to bloom,
Will find its joy in this green room.

In the Company of Elegance

Sipping tea with a fern so wise,
Laughing at clouds and sunny skies.
Roses recount their love affairs,
While daisies giggle in their chairs.

The drapes of ivy softly sway,
As trumpets play to greet the day.
A posy snickers at garden gnomes,
While thorns plot to steal their homes.

Each petal's tale brings hearty cheer,
In floral riddles, nothing to fear.
Together in this flowery chat,
Who knew plants were such aristocrats?

A Heart Entwined in Green

In pots of dreams, I plant my soul,
Each petal's dance, a funny goal.
With leaves that giggle, twisting tight,
My heart's a jungle, what a sight!

Sunshine spills its laughter bright,
As blooms play peekaboo at night.
I water them with silly songs,
Yet wonder if this love belongs.

Tangled vines with cheerful grins,
They poke my thoughts where fun begins.
In this green maze where joy blooms wide,
Are they my friends or just my pride?

With every sprout, a new delight,
I prance around in pure delight.
Life's too short for serious schemes,
Let's shout and laugh among the greens!

Tapestry of Fragile Sighs

A dance of colors, soft and bright,
These delicate blooms bring pure delight.
Yet with each sip of morning dew,
I trip on petals, but who knew?

They whisper secrets, oh so sly,
As I weave dreams beneath the sky.
With flowers perched upon my head,
I strut around like I'm well-bred.

These poetic blooms can make me trip,
But watch me now, I'll take a dip!
In the fragrant chaos of this spree,
Sighs of joy are wild and free.

So let's embrace this tangled bliss,
With every flower and silly kiss.
A tapestry woven in pure fun,
Where fragile sighs can dance and run!

Blooming Moments of Longing

A blooper reel of nature's grace,
Each petal hides a silly face.
In moments sweet, I find my charm,
Yet bruise a bud, alarm! Alarm!

I long to capture joy in bloom,
But tripping over roots, I fume.
The sly buds giggle, oh so coy,
They sprout the tales of my lost joy.

Each twist and turn, a vibrant laugh,
In this greenhouse, I'm the daft staff.
With every bloom, a moment pure,
Yet watch your step, that's for sure!

Riding on the breeze of dreams,
In this garden's funny schemes.
I bloom with glee, a giggling sprite,
Creating moments, pure delight!

In the Shade of the Whispering Leaves

Beneath the leaves where whispers play,
I find my joy at close of day.
With shadows stretching, laughter hides,
In that cool shade, my heart abides.

The plants conspire with nature's flair,
To tickle my whims, a breezy air.
I chase their giggles, lost in the fun,
In this leafy realm, laughter's spun.

Each leaf a secret, kept in jest,
As I tumble 'neath this leafy fest.
They sway and sway, my giggling crew,
Under the sun with its golden hue.

Though nature's voice may tease and play,
With every chuckle, I'll find my way.
In this haven beneath the trees,
Life's sweetest moments are all with ease!

Fractal Patterns of Passion

In pots of clay where dreams collide,
Petals dance, then slip and slide.
An artist's brush of hues and shades,
Creating chaos in my glades.

A careful garden, how it blooms,
I talk to flowers, hear their tunes.
They roll their eyes, I swear they do,
While sipping dew and chasing blue.

With every stem, a tale is spun,
In secret chats, we laugh for fun.
They tease my choices, point and jest,
But beauty rhymes with no contest.

Each leaf a joke, each stem a laugh,
I sketch the grace in tangled path.
With every bloom, they draw me near,
These floral friends, my giggle cheer.

The Blooming Soul

In vibrant hues, I lose my mind,
What louder shouts than petals aligned?
They flaunt their colors, oh so bright,
As I pour tea and hold on tight.

I wear a crown of green and gold,
These blooms are stories yet untold.
They wink at me when no one sees,
Great fun is grown with each new breeze.

With laughter loud, they twist and sway,
A secret dance they crave each day.
While prancing round, I join the spree,
Who knew a plant could be so free?

So here I stand, with blooms in tow,
Their cheerful sprawl my heart's tableau.
In every petal, giggles swell,
In nature's laugh, we weave our spell.

Symphonies of Color

Amidst the blooms, a concert's found,
With rustling leaves, the laughter's sound.
Petals pluck the strings of glee,
In this garden, wild and free.

The yellow blooms croon notes so bright,
While violets strum through day and night.
Each swirl of color, a cheeky jest,
In nature's play, we are all blessed.

The blushing rose sings soft and low,
To daisies dancing in a row.
And while they play, I laugh along,
In this vibrant life, we all belong.

So come, dear friend, join in the tune,
Where flowers laugh beneath the moon.
Their colors wrap the world in cheer,
With every note, the heart draws near.

Veins of Exquisite Grace

In twisted paths where petals grow,
I've stumbled on a quirky show.
The leaves converse with playful grace,
In this lively floral space.

With every vine, a new embrace,
They tickle thoughts, a floral chase.
From dainty buds to blooms so bold,
A wild adventure 'twixt petals told.

In sunlight's glow, they wink and play,
With laughter bright, they steal the day.
Each part a story, woven tight,
A tapestry of pure delight.

So here we laugh in colors bright,
As flowers dance in morning light.
In nature's whims, we find our place,
With silly blooms, we've made our case.

Blooming in a Silent World

In a garden of colors, I sneak,
Petals giggle, they're playing hide and seek.
My clumsy feet trip over a vine,
That's the last time I'll dance with a sign.

A bee buzzes loudly, thinks he's the boss,
But I wave my arms, don't care what's lost.
Each flower's a tale, that's waiting to bloom,
"Look at me!" they scream, "Can we get some room?"

I planted my dreams with a shovel and glee,
But ended up growing a topiary tree.
It's not what I pictured, but hey, it's alright,
I still prefer laughter over being uptight.

So here in this jungle, with laughter and cheer,
I'll chat with the tulips, no humans near.
Who needs conversations with boring old folks,
When petals around me giggle like jokes?

Fading into a Spectrum

Colors collide in a floral parade,
Dancing around with a graceful charade.
But when I show up, all bright and immense,
I'm the David to their Goliath — intense!

The petals start blushing, shy as can be,
I'm here to brighten your day, can't you see?
Yet all that they do is wobble and sway,
I'm trying to help, but what do they say?

"Could you tone it down? We're delicate blooms,"
But I laugh and reply, "I'll explode in your rooms!"
With a flash of my personality bright,
Who needs conventions when you've got true light?

So here we go, a riot of hue,
My loudness fades gently, I promise, it's true.
As colors entwine in a fanciful way,
Let's bloom together, come join my melee!

The Heartbeats of Flora

In a patch of bright green, I spy my new crush,
A flower so lovely, it makes my heart rush.
But, alas, I stumble, my balance is out,
Falling flat on my face, no fuzz, just a pout.

The daisies are snickering, can't hold back their glee,
"What a silly human, so messy and free!"
Though I'm often the joke, I don't really mind,
In this floral circus, my heart's tightly entwined.

Who knew blooms had stories, so raucous and loud?
Petal gossip floats, like a floral crowd.
If flowers could talk, oh the tales they'd weave,
About playful mischief, their laughter, I believe.

So treasured are moments stitched into the green,
With the heartbeat of nature, a rhythm unseen.
Let's giggle together, let petals entwine,
In the vibrant embrace of this fun, sweet design.

Jewel-Toned Whispers

In the garden of sparkles, a treasure I see,
A dazzling delight whispering just to me.
With colors that shimmer like jewels in the night,
I can't keep a straight face; it's pure, silly delight.

A bloom waves its petals, "Come dance in the dew!"
I twirl in response, with a wink, "How about you?"
But I trip on a root, oh, what a funny sight,
The flowers all giggle; they think I'm just light.

Each bud has a secret, a laugh in its core,
They nudge one another, "What's she falling for?"
It's hard to keep straight when nature's this spry,
When every step forward feels like a fly.

So here's to the whispers, the giggles, the cheer,
In this garden of wonders, there's nothing to fear.
With jewels and laughter, life's sweet energy,
I'll embrace every bloom, it's just you and me!

Enigmas of the Fern-Filled Nook

In a fern-filled nook, oh what a sight,
A plant in a pot feels quite alright.
It struts with flair, a leafy delight,
Whispers of grandeur, day and night.

With friends all around, it throws a ball,
Where ferns and greens heed the call.
In this merry space, no one is small,
Just nature's dance, we love it all.

There's laughter in leaves, a giggle or two,
Plants jiving to tunes only they knew.
A party of petals in dazzling hue,
Who knew botany had such fun, it's true!

So join this parade, oh don't be shy,
With ferns and fancies that touch the sky.
In this enchanting nook, we'll laugh and sigh,
As greens have fun, let's give it a try!

Surrender to the Botanic.

In the garden's grip, I twirl and sway,
Amidst the blooms, I dance and play.
With every sprout, I'm led astray,
Whisked into joy—it's a plant buffet!

What's this one here? A curious hybrid,
Its petals shout out, 'You're not a kid!'
It tickles my nose, and then it slid,
But I chuckle along, what a wild bid!

The leaves hold secrets, or so they claim,
A hint of chaos in the floral game.
Each episode feels a bit the same,
Yet I can't help but giggle at their fame.

So join me, friend, let's lose our way,
In a landscape of blooms, let's dance and sway.
Surrender your heart, just laugh, don't stay,
For botanic mischief is here to play!

Petals of Enchantment

Hiding in petals, dreams take flight,
Each bloom a giggle, pure delight.
With colors that shimmer, oh what a sight,
They whisper sweet nothings, day and night.

In this forest of flora, we chase the sun,
Playing with shadows, oh what fun!
With frolicking bees that buzz and run,
In a realm where silly is never done.

What's that bloom over there? A riddle to solve,
Like 'Where is the cheese?' in a floral dissolve!
It sways and it jiggles, our hearts it involves,
In this garden of giggles, we're heroes resolved.

So dance with the petals, a whimsical spree,
With laughter and wonders, come share with me.
In this realm of enchantment, wild and free,
Every bloom holds a joke—just wait and see!

Whispered Secrets in Bloom

In a world of color, secrets unwind,
Petals sing softly, and oh, how they bind.
With gossip of flowers, both sweet and kind,
Each hushed revelation is quite a find.

Underneath the leaves, a chuckle occurs,
Between blooms, laughter gently stirs.
A joke on the breeze, oh how it purrs,
Life in the garden surely concurs!

With petals as gossipers, bold and bright,
They share with us tales of sheer delight.
In this sunny patch, spirits take flight,
As the flowers of fun bask in the light.

So lean in close, hear the whispers near,
For nature has secrets, that much is clear.
In this blossoming world, let's all cheer,
In the joy of the garden, we conquer our fear!

Petal-Paved Pathways

In gardens where colors clash and play,
Petals dance in a breezy sway.
Bees wear tiny hats, it's quite absurd,
Each flower whispers, 'Have you heard?'

A plucky bloom, with a sparkle bright,
Jokes about colors, oh what a sight!
'Why so serious, green leaf, my friend?
Let's twist and turn, and not pretend!'

Daisies giggle, roses roll their eyes,
While sunflowers boast of their sunny skies.
The lilies laugh with such flair and grace,
As petals twirl in a flower race!

In this garden, all worries cease,
With a fragrant breeze, we find our peace.
So come on down, let laughter unfurl,
Among these blooms, the quirkiest world!

Velveteen Vows

Under violet skies, love blooms anew,
Each petal holds secrets, strange but true.
Roses write vows in shades of the night,
While daisies doodle, a comical sight.

'I promise to tickle and make you giggle,
To dance in the wind, and sometimes wiggle!'
Said the velveteen blooms with flair and jest,
'In this garden of laughter, we're truly blessed!'

The tulips declare with a vibrant shout,
'What's love without petals? Yeah, we'll sort it out!'
Each stem holds a story, some zany, some wise,
In vibrant hues beneath the sunny skies.

So let's toast with nectar, a love so sweet,
Where pollen and laughter joyfully meet.
In this land of blooms, where jokes abound,
Velveteen vows in the garden are found!

Dreams in Lavender Hues

In fields of lavender, dreams swirl and sway,
Each velvet petal dreams of play.
Bees wear shades, they're stylin' and cool,
Planning wild parties, oh what a fool!

While butterflies sip on nectar divine,
They giggle and gossip about the sunshine.
'What if we danced on a daisy's head?
Or tried to hop on clouds instead?'

The whispers of flowers float on the breeze,
While giggles travel among the trees.
Dreams in hues of purple abound,
With laughter echoing, all around.

So let's dive deep in this fragrant sea,
Where whimsy and mischief are wild and free.
In lavender dreams, we'll happily roam,
In a world where flowers feel right at home!

Silken Hues and Heartstrings

With silken hues, the blooms take flight,
Heartstrings tugging with sheer delight.
Petals chuckle, sparking joy anew,
While stems sway softly, like a dance crew.

Frogs in bow ties croak with flair,
'The dandelions are looking debonair!'
While violets tease with a wink and grin,
'With heartstrings twirling, let the fun begin!'

In a garden party with laughter loud,
Flowers strut proudly, oh my, they're cowed.
Each petal a note in a merry tune,
Swaying beneath the big fat moon.

So gather around, let the merry-go-round,
With silken hues and joy abound.
As hearts entwine in this floral show,
In the garden of wonders, let the smiles grow!

Petals of Enchantment

In a garden where laughter grows,
Dancing petals strike silly poses.
They twirl and skip, oh what a sight,
With colors that giggle in the sunlight.

A daisy tried flirting, oh dear me,
But the roses rolled their eyes with glee.
Tulips teased, 'We've got the flair!'
While pansies just acted like they don't care.

In this carnival of leafy delight,
The sunflowers cheered with all their might.
While stems wiggled and leaves did sway,
This floral fiesta brightened the day.

So here we gather, a merry crew,
With petals that wink and giggle too.
Let's seize the blooms, oh what a chance,
For in this garden, we all can dance!

Whispers in Bloom

When buds start chatting, oh what a thrill,
They whisper secrets, louder still.
'Look at that bee, isn't he bold?'
'Just don't mention the gardener's hold!'

A lilac said, 'I'm feeling quite grand!'
While daisies made dibs on the bandstand.
They sang of sunshine and sweet summer rain,
While petunias giggled with barely contained grain.

Amongst the blooms, the gossip flows,
With silly tales only flora knows.
A lily laughed, 'I just lost a petal!'
'But you're still fabulous!'—a cheeky mettle!

So join the uproar where flowers confide,
They're bound to make you beam with pride.
For in this lush riot, joy's on display,
And the petals all join in the fun-fueled play!

The Language of Petals

In whispers soft, petals declare,
Words of wonder float in the air.
The tulips laugh as they teach the ways,
Of flirty gazes and colorful praise.

A daffodil shouts, 'I'm a sunny star!'
While violets sigh, 'You've gone too far!'
They debate with flair on who blooms best,
While bees note down their lively jest.

Petals invented a game called 'Tag',
Where petals plunge with a little brag.
'You can't catch me,' giggle the greens,
While snickering leaves disrupt all the scenes.

So take a moment, lean in to hear,
The floral antics that bring us cheer.
In this petal parlance, fun reigns supreme,
And blooming friendships now stitch the seam!

Shadows of the Exotic

In the shadows where the weird things bloom,
Strange plants giggle, weaving a loom.
With colors so wild, they give quite a scare,
But dance in the moonlight, oh what a flare!

Cacti jive with spikes like hairdos,
While ferns throw shade in their funky shoes.
They come together for nights in the dark,
With laughter that echoes, a floral spark.

An oddball vine claims it's tightrope skill,
While lilies just chill with a glamorous thrill.
Despite their quirks, friendships bloom tight,
In this shadowed garden, all feels so right.

So tiptoe with joy in this zany retreat,
Where every petal hums to a whimsical beat.
In the dance of the exotic, hilarity sings,
Amongst the flora, today's joy springs!

Reverie in Rosy Hues

In a pot where colors dance,
A pink delight, a silly chance.
I named her Grace, she likes to sway,
And giggles when I pass her way.

She whispers sweet, 'Do rags be gone!'
Her petals fluffed, she loves the dawn.
Yet when I water, oh what a sight!
She splashes back, oh, what a fright!

Tiny bugs, they try to sneak,
My floral babe, she plays hide and seek.
With every bloom, her antics soar,
I brace myself, what's next in store?

In rosy hues, our laughter spins,
She ticks and tocks, where mischief begins.
With every petal, a raucous cheer,
Together we bloom, let's hoot and jeer!

Captive in Jardins Secrets

In secret gardens, mischief brews,
I giggle at the fragrant cues.
Each bloom a tale, a playful spark,
In leafy realms, we dance till dark.

She lifts her head, in playful jest,
'Who knew plants could really jest?'
I nod in mirth, as bees align,
Their buzzing tunes, a silly whine.

A squirrel in shades of vibrant hues,
Chases the blooms, oh what a ruse!
I toss a seed, but it's a trap,
He slips and slides—hey! Must be a lap!

In the shadows, we chuckle loud,
Our leafy friends, we're quite the crowd.
A garden full of jest and cheer,
Life's funniest quirks, yes, they are near!

In the Company of Smooth Petals

With smooth petals, she's quite the queen,
Always adorned in shimmering green.
Her laughter rings like chimes in breeze,
A floral friend, she aims to please.

Yet when the sun begins to shine,
She poses sweet, oh how divine!
Distracted by the sunlit gleam,
She forgets to sip—how can this be a dream?

A gentle poke, her petal sways,
Together we laugh through sunny days.
Each bloom a treasure, each bud a jest,
In our floral realm, we're truly blessed.

With smooth petals, oh what a scene,
She's the fairest in all the green.
In every bloom, our joy confides,
Best friends forever, where fun abides!

The Garden's Silent Confession

In whispers low, the garden sighs,
Secrets float beneath the skies.
Each stem, a tale, a funny plot,
Where blooms conspire in every spot.

One day I found a cheeky sprout,
'Oh dear,' it seemed, 'You've got it out!'
A ticklish laugh, it shook and swayed,
A garden full of mischief made.

The daisies giggled, the roses sneered,
While violets whispered, 'We are not feared!'
A world of whimsy, colors bright,
In every bud, pure delight ignites.

The garden's hush, a secret song,
Where every bloom just plays along.
In silent confessions, laughter grows,
And every petal, a joke that glows!

The Allure of Ephemeral Beauty

In a garden of whispers, blooms sway,
Tiny faces dance, keeping gloom at bay.
They wink in the sun, flaunting their flair,
With spots and stripes, they have flair to spare.

A petal parade, dressed in bright hues,
Each one declares, 'I'm the star of the news!'
With charm in the breeze, they tickle our noses,
But watch where you step, those thorns give you poses!

They come and they go, like a fleeting joke,
A laugh in the breeze, when sunshine awoke.
They flirt with our hearts, then bid their adieu,
Leaving us puzzled: "What happened to you?"

Yet in every bloom, there's a tale to unfold,
Of laughter and dreams, and the brave and the bold.
So here's to the blooms, that bring cheeky cheer,
In the garden of life, let's hold them all dear!

Caught in Flora's Embrace

Amidst the green thicket, a giggle erupts,
A floral conspiracy, oh how it disrupts!
The petals conspire in colorful plots,
While leaves eavesdrop, spinning their thoughts.

A flower's a joker, with petals that grin,
With a flamboyant twist, they tug at our chin.
The bees start the buzz, the butterflies tease,
As they swirl through the air, doing 'as they please'.

Oh, what a circus, this bloom-filled spree,
Each flower a jester, wild and carefree.
They chuckle together, their secrets combined,
In their vibrant cabaret, laughter entwined.

Caught in this charm, we join in the fun,
With roots in the earth, we dance in the sun.
So let's raise a toast, to these prankster delights,
In the arms of the blooms, our heart takes flight!

Epidendrum Echoes

Here blooms a tale, of color and cheer,
An Epidendrum giggles, oh so near!
With every rustle, it whispers and sighs,
As the garden's own troubadour, under blue skies.

In polka dot socks, it frolics around,
With pals made of petals, in freedom unbound.
They plot to confuse, with a dance so absurd,
A floral fiesta, it's utterly stirred!

The sunshine's a spotlight, the clouds their applause,
As they twirl and they leap, with great pomp and cause.
Each bloom takes a bow, with a wink and a laugh,
"Join us in this jest, join our floral giraffe!"

So sip on the nectar of joy they impart,
These tricks from the petals, that brighten the heart.
In the echo of petals, such giggles remain,
As long as there's laughter, we dance in the rain!

Velvet Petals at Dusk

When the sun sets low, a velvet display,
The blooms gather 'round, in a cheeky ballet.
With soft little whispers, in twilight's embrace,
They share their wild tales, each follows their pace.

A rogue petal twirls, with a wink and a spin,
Flirting with shadows, where mischief begins.
The dusk giggles softly, as colors collide,
In this velvety charm, we happily glide.

Fate puts on a show, with these silly delights,
Every bloom has a story, that dances in lights.
With laughter and glances, the petals confide,
In the hush of the night, their secrets abide.

So let's toast to the dusk, where the blossoms unite,
In a velvet embrace, beneath stars shining bright.
Together they laugh, in soft moonlit shrouds,
In a world full of wonder, where joy always crowds!

Dreaming in Petal Hues

In the garden, quite absurd,
Colors dance, and laughter's stirred.
Petals blow, they tease the sun,
Whispering tales of floral fun.

Bee in a tux, collecting gold,
Sipping nectar, he's quite bold.
Butterflies wear fancy hats,
Two-step next to playful cats.

Silly stems start to prance,
Dancing roots in joyous trance.
Nature's circus, don't you see?
Come join this wild jubilee!

Colors pop in every glance,
Behind each leaf, there's a chance.
To giggle at what blooms anew,
In every petal, a laugh or two!

The Hidden Pulse of Nature

Under the leaves, whispers flow,
Roots tickle soil, just for show.
Worms in suits, they shimmy about,
While ants throw a tiny shout.

Crickets chirp a silly tune,
Beneath the bright and watchful moon.
Frogs croak jokes without a heed,
While flowers giggle, quite freed!

The breeze delivers tales so sweet,
Of bumbles on their sticky feet.
Everything's buzzing with delight,
Nature's funny, day and night.

Embark on this whimsical quest,
Where petals laugh and roots invest.
Join the critters for a spin,
In this sport, let joy begin!

Enchantment in Every Leaf

In the glade where giggles grow,
Leaves shake hands, put on a show.
Tiny sprites with gleeful glee,
Painted wings flit joyfully.

Petal pals in colors rare,
Trade silly jokes in the warm air.
Dewdrops laugh as they collide,
Creating moments fun and wide.

Amongst the blooms, chaos reigns,
Bees lose track, but never feign.
Every stem has something grand,
In this vibrant, goofy land.

So come, dear friend, and take a look,
Nature's tales hide in each nook.
With laughter stitched in every leaf,
You'll find joy beyond belief!

The Breath of the Blossoms

A breeze whispers secrets to each bloom,
Tickling petals within their room.
Petals puff, they catch a breeze,
Sharing smiles among the trees.

Hummingbirds in quite a race,
Zooming by with candy grace.
"Your nectar's sweet, but I must dash!"
They giggle, then they're gone in a flash!

The blooms all chuckle, what a sight,
Colors mix in pure delight.
With laughter wrapped in fragrant air,
Nature's joy is everywhere!

A breeze tousles every hair,
And petals dance without a care.
So take a moment, pause and sigh,
In this funny land, oh my!

Elegy for an Elusive Bloom

In shadows deep, she plays hide and seek,
A flower so rare, yet not a word to speak.
With petals like whispers and a fragrance so sly,
She giggles away, just a fluttered goodbye.

I searched through the jungle, I climbed every hill,
But she danced from my grasp, with a mischievous thrill.
Each time I reach for her, she twirls out of view,
I'm left with a fern, what's a gardener to do?

I'll bribe with a watering can full of sweet tea,
Or maybe she fancies a game of charades with me.
In this floral fiesta, my heart skips a beat,
Who knew planting dreams could be such a feat?

But fret not, dear bloom, I shall find you someday,
With chocolates and petals, let's laugh the night away.
For you're just a petal, and I'll keep you in sight,
Until then, I'll nurse this absurd gardener's plight.

Tints of Temptation

Painting the garden in colors so bright,
A splash of allure that sparks sheer delight.
She wears her hues boldly, with a wink and a nod,
While I stand here blushing, looking quite odd.

With pinks that are sweet and reds like a sin,
Each shade tempts my heart, and I just can't win.
I've mixed my own palette, but it's all gone awry,
With blues that look green and yellows that cry.

She swirls in the breeze with a confident stance,
While I'm tripping over my own sprightly plants.
Her petals shout "Look! Make your friends all envious!"
But I just grow weeds, so they're feeling pity for us.

Yet still, I adore her, this diva of blooms,
With laughter and joy, she brightens my rooms.
Forever I'll try, with my brush and my jest,
To capture her essence, at my humorous best.

Garden Reverie by Moonlight

Under moon's watch, the garden does gleam,
Whispering secrets, a wild, silly dream.
The blooms are all giggling, with sparkles of dew,
While I dance like a rabbit—oh, what a sight too!

Stars play along like a mischievous crowd,
As I'm waltzing with petals, feeling quite proud.
But watch your step, dear friend, it's a dangerous game,
I tripped on a root, and oh, what a shame!

In this soft glow, each flower's a star,
But, of course, they're laughing—my moves are bizarre.
I bow to the daisies, parade with the ferns,
But they giggle and whisper, "Let's wait for his turns!"

Yet, joy fills the air, amidst laughter and fun,
As blooms twirl and twist, till the rise of the sun.
With each nightly frolic, sweet dreams come alive,
In this moonlit garden, where chuckling thrives.

Lush Revelations

In the lushest retreat, where the colors collide,
I ponder life's riddles, with blooms by my side.
But every discovery just leads me to giggle,
Why do these petals prance and wiggle?

They tease and they taunt, like jester's delight,
With blossoms that shout, "Come on, join our plight!"
Each succulent moment is a jest in disguise,
While bees buzz in chorus, plotting costume surprise.

I thought I was wise, an expert in blooms,
But my plants seem to know all my secrets and dooms.
They dance in the sunlight, with petals so bold,
While I'm left in stitches, feeling quite old.

Oh what a garden, a whimsical place,
With secrets and laughter, life's joyful embrace.
So here's to the blossoms, with charms they impart,
For in their lush revelry, lies the fun in the heart.

www.ingramcontent.com/pod-product-compliance
Lightning Source LLC
Chambersburg PA
CBHW070333120526
44590CB00017B/2869